Out of School

What do you do when away from school? Climb trees, play games, go skating, go fishing . . . ? There are so many things to do out of school and these poems are all about them.

Cover illustration by Desmond Clover

Out of School

An Anthology of Poems
compiled by
Dennis Saunders

Illustrations by Desmond Clover

Evans Brothers Limited London

Published by Evans Brothers Limited
Montague House, Russell Square,
London, W.C.1.

First published 1972
Third printing 1973

Set in 11 on 12pt Baskerville
and printed in Great Britain by
Cox and Wyman Limited,
London, Reading and Fakenham
CSD ISBN 0 237 35109 9
PB ISBN 0 237 35110 2 PRA 3467

Contents

Wishes

Acknowledgements

For permission to use copyright material the editor and publishers are indebted to the following:

The Bodley Head for 'Going Downhill on a Bicycle' by H. C. Beeching and, with Dodd, Mead and Company, Inc., 'I Meant to Do My Work Today' from *The Lonely Dancer* by Richard le Gallienne; Jonathan Cape Ltd, and Holt, Rinehart & Winston, Inc., for the extract from 'Birches' from *The Poetry of Robert Frost*; the author and Chatto & Windus Ltd. for 'Alex at the Barber's' from *Fairground Music* by John Fuller; the proprietors of *Child Life* for 'I Held a Lamb' by Kim Worthington; The Cresset Press for 'The Boy Fishing' from *The River Steamer* by E. J. Scovell; The Daily Mirror for 'The Cave' by Christopher Fairbairn and 'Saturday' by Barbara Merritt; Faber & Faber Ltd. for 'My Brother Bert' from *Meet My Folks* by Ted Hughes and 'Child on Top of a Greenhouse' from *The Collected Poems of Theodore Roethke*; Rupert Hart-Davies for 'A Child's Voice' from *Quiet as Moss* by Andrew Young; William Heinemann Ltd. for 'Skating' from *Pillicock Hill* by Herbert Asquith, 'Little Fan' from *The Wandering Moon* by James Reeves and 'The Giant Crab' from *The Truants* by John Walsh; David Higham Associates Ltd. for 'There Isn't Time' and 'It was a Long Time Ago' from *Silver, Sand and Snow*, and The Literary Trustees of Walter de la Mare and The Society of Authors for 'High' from *The Complete Poems of Walter de la Mare*; MacGibbon & Kee and Harcourt, Brace Jovanovich, Inc., for 'maggie and milly and molly and may' from *The Complete Poems of e. e. cummings*; Macmillan & Co Ltd. for 'House of Sand' from

Coming Out Fighting by Philip Hobsbaum; The Macmillan Company, New York for 'Tree-Sleeping' by Robert P. Tristram Coffin; the North West Arts Association for 'Heat Wave' by Valerie Hodge; Oxford University Press for 'Mick' from *The Blackbird in the Lilac* by James Reeves, 'Anne and the Fieldmouse' from *Happily Ever After* and 'Suzanne at the Hairdresser's' from *The Tale of the Monster Horse* by Ian Serraillier; the author for 'Any Excuse' by T. H. Parker; Rand, McNally and Company for 'Halloween' by Marie A. Lawson; the author for 'Hide and Seek' from *Walking Wounded* by Vernon Scannell; the author for 'The Wind at Night' by David Shavreen; Mrs. Starkey for 'The Piper' by Seamus O'Sullivan; the author for 'Canoe Story' and 'Windy Boy in a Windswept Tree' by Geoffrey Summerfield; the author for 'Out of School' by Hal Summers; the author for 'The Calendar' by Barbara Euphan Todd; the Trustees of the Tagore Estate and Macmillan & Co. Ltd. for 'Day by Day I Float My Paper Boats' and 'I Wish I Were. . .' by Rabindranath Tagore; the author for 'Five O'Clock Tea' by Steven Willett; World's Work Ltd. for 'If Once You Have Slept on an Island' and 'Meeting' from *Taxis and Toadstools* by Rachel Field and, with Grosset & Dunlap Inc., 'Old Man Ocean' from *The Pedalling Man* by Russell Hoban.

For Clare

About these poems

This is a collection of poems about some of the things you do when you're out of school: playing games, at home or in the street, fishing by the river or crabbing on the seashore, exploring strange places, enjoying your pets, canoeing and skating and skipping and climbing trees. Yes, and even *sleeping* in trees, according to one of the poets. I'm afraid I was one of those boys who usually slipped rather than slept in trees, and felt very much as the boy feels in Geoffrey Summerfield's poem *Windy Boy in a Windswept Tree*. In fact, I still remember the bruises! Still, in *Tree-Sleeping* the poet does admit that the spruce had 'boughs like beds' that prevented him from falling. On the whole the trees *I* climbed were oak and elm, and far less comfortable than spruce.

Not all the poems are about everyday happenings. Some are concerned with day dreaming, playing the game of 'I wish . . .' as Robert Louis Stevenson does in his poem *Travel*. This is something I'm sure we all do, both in and out of school. And most of us know someone like Bert whose hobby is collecting animals as pets. But what would happen if the hobby got completely out of hand? Ted Hughes toys with the idea of 'What if . . .?' and comes up with some very amusing results.

'Let's pretend' is fun, but even quite ordinary experiences can be made interesting and exciting when captured in a poem. For instance, have *you* ever lain in bed at night listening to the howling of the wind? Read David Shavreen's poem *The Wind at Night* and notice how he sees the wind in his imagination – as a train, as yelling bandits, as thudding hooves. Ian Serraillier takes a commonplace event, too – the visit to the hairdresser – and makes us see it as if for the first time. You see, you don't need to invent things to write about to be a poet. Poets write about the things they see happening around them, and the things they hear and feel. Anything that catches your interest and amuses you or excites you can be your subject.

You will see that I have included several poems by quite young writers. Steven Willett tells us about tea-time in his home, Valerie Hodge recalls the sleepiness of a hot lazy afternoon out of doors, while Richard Alan Pierce has taken the apparently unpromising subject of an ordinary village pond and make a striking and faintly sinister little poem from it.

I hope, then, that you enjoy these poems and, having read them, why don't *you* have a go? Write about some out-of-school activity that particularly interests you, and be absolutely honest in what you write. Always say what you really feel and describe what you really see and hear. And don't forget to send a copy of your poem to me. I'd like to see it, very much.

Dennis Saunders

OUT OF SCHOOL

Saturday

I waved to dog and Dad
Getting unwilling cows. Nigger had
Chased a lazy mottled heifer
Through the mud encircled gate.

I swung on the old swing,
Its unoiled hooks screeching, sing
To birds and sky and noise
Of cars and cricket over the hedge.

I squeezed through the garden gate
Where a lilac breathes its lofty hate
Over tall nettles and broad docks,
Dandelions and tough goose grass.

Barbara Merritt, aged 13

Out of School

Four o'clock strikes,
There's a rising hum,
Then the doors fly open,
The children come.

With a wild cat-call
And a hop-scotch hop
And a bouncing ball
And a whirling top,

Grazing of knees,
A hair-pull and a slap,
A hitched-up satchel,
A pulled-down cap,

Bully boys reeling off,
Hurt ones squealing off,
Aviators wheeling off,
Mousy ones stealing off,

Woollen gloves for chilblains,
Cotton rags for snufflers,
Pigtails, coat-tails,
Tails of mufflers,

Machine-gun cries,
A kennelful of snarlings
A hurricane of leaves,
A treeful of starlings,

Thinning away now
By some and some,
Thinning away, away,
All gone home.

Hal Summers

Two in Bed

When my brother Tommy
Sleeps in bed with me,
He doubles up
And makes
himself
exactly
like
a
V
And 'cause the bed is not so wide,
A part of him is on my side.

Abram Bunn Ross

Urchin

Sing a song o' somersaults,
A pocket full o' conkers.
Betty Jane's in bed again
Wiv pimples on 'er blinkers.
Blimey, there's a copper there!
Watch yer step, me 'earty.
Only wants the vicar 'ere
To make it quite a party.
Shut up, Roddie. 'Ave a care,
'E'll put you on 'is roll-call.
Give 'im socks? I wouldn't dare.
'E'd pop me down the coal-'ole.

Sing a song o' fourpence,
Sixpence by-and-by.
Four and twenty roller-skates
Zoomin' down the High.
Phew! wot a caboodleum!
Watch out for yer poodle, mum.
It's Alf and little Roddie.
'Old tight, mind yer backs!
You can keep yer Cadillacs.
We're comin'! everybody!

Christopher Hassall

Alex at the Barber's *(an extract)*

He is having his hair cut. Towels are tucked
About his chin, his mop scalped jokingly.
The face in the mirror is his own face.

The barber moves and chats among the green
And methylated violet, snipper-snips,
Puts scissors down, puts in a plaited flex,

And like a surgeon with his perfumed hands
Presses the waiting skull and shapes the base.
He likes having his hair cut, and the man

Likes cutting it. The radio drones on.
The eyes in the mirror are his own eyes.
While the next chair receives the Demon Blade,

A dog-leg razor nicks a sideburn here;
As from a sofa there a sheet is whisked
And silver pocketed. The doorbell pings.

The barber, frowning, grips the ragged fringe
And slowly cuts. Upon the speckled sheet
The bits fall down and now his hair is cut.

John Fuller

Suzanne at the Hairdresser's

Robed in white on a lofty throne
I sit before the mirror, alone.

Snip, snip! the scissors clap,
heaping gold upon my lap.

Alone, did I say? there's another me
in the mirror to keep me company

And watch the stray wispy locks
like hours from dandelion clocks

Floating down the sunny air.
You'd never think it was my hair!

How hot and still the morning seems,
a day for half-shut eyes and dreams.

Now the mirror round's a pool;
I peer from out the water cool,

Hands and curly head and face –
all is hid below my waist.

What lies below? Perhaps the scales
of a mermaid's twinkling tail.

Ian Serraillier

Child on Top of a Greenhouse

The wind billowing out the seat of my britches,
My feet crackling splinters of glass and dried putty,
The half-grown chrysanthemums staring up like
  accusers,
Up through the streaked glass, flashing with sunlight,
A few white clouds all rushing eastward,
A line of elms plunging and tossing like horses,
And everyone, everyone pointing up and shouting!

Theodore Roethke

Windy Boy in a Windswept Tree

The branch swayed, swerved,
Swept and whipped, up,
Down, right to left,
Then leapt to the right again,
As if to hurl him down
To smash to smithereens
On the knife-edged grass
Or smother
In the close-knit quilts of moss.
Out on a crazy limb
He screwed his eyes tight shut,
To keep out the dizzy ground.
Sweat greased his palms;
Fear pricked his forehead.
The twisted branches lunged and lurched,
His body curved, twisted, he arched
His legs and gripped the bark
Between his ankles.
The crust of the bark
Sharp as glasspaper
And rough with wrinkles
Grazed his skin
And raised the raw red flesh
And crazed his mind
With fear of breaking.
Then the mad-cap, capering wind
Dropped.
The branch steadied.
Paused,
Rested.

He slowly clambered, slowly, back,
Slowly so safely,
Then dropped
Like a wet blanket
To the rock-like, reassuring ground.
Finally, without a sound,
He walked carefully
Home.

Geoffrey Summerfield

The Wind at Night

The dustbin lids clang on the ground,
The tree tops groan,
The wind down the bedroom chimney
Begins to moan.
I hear a sudden roar
Through the blankets covering my face,
The clatter and rattle of wheels
At a furious pace;
It's the Union Express, the Iron Steed,
Rumbling across the prairies
At breakneck speed.

It pounds through the chimney stacks.
Screams to a halt,
Stops in its tracks.

Silence follows.
Then with a hiss
The airy train
Accelerates again,
Thundering along the housetops
With shrieks and bellows.
Racing across the plains,
It splashes through mud and mire,
Out-stripping the painted redskins,
Their arrows fierce as fire;
Outwitting the train-wreckers,
Men masked and mean with greed,
With a fierce burst of steam
And a triumphant rattle of speed.

And the Indians wail and howl
Raising their cry of despair
As the rear-lamp swings into darkness,
And the train melts into air.
And the bandits shout their curses
After their vanished prey,
Till the oaths echo wild round the roofs,
And the thudding of horses' hoofs
Flying, dying away,
Grows still, and silence deep
At last brings calm
And sleep.

David Shavreen

The Cave

Boom! went the echoing sound
Of a foot hitting the side of the dark
Eerie place of a phantom.
A cave. The two-sided tunnel that led
For at first only thirty yards inwards.

But that contains an old spider,
Whose web stretched half way across
The entrance to the cave.
Then there came the old, so old –
Was he the adder? The brown
Stripes lined his slimy back with
Camouflage for the deadly strike
On the spider, who cautiously watched him.

Of course we had the old frog,
Who had seen even the adder's egg.
Who lurked in the weeds and grass of the
Big puddle that had never dried up.
Then years later the cave will stretch
Even farther and there will be another
Adder, another frog and another spider
Who are all eerier than the last.

Christopher Michael Fairbairn, aged 12

The Pond

In the breeze a beautiful pond shimmers and flitters.
A trickle of water runs by. A flitter – a frog starts
Gurgling away in a funny language.
Plop! A stick falls from a tree,
The water spreads and curls like a
Catherine wheel. A reed flaps and winds over
The water's edge, it reflects on the water.
On the surface of the water lies a whole
Countryside. The trees shudder. A log races
Past. The water is green of mould,
The grit is disturbed by a fish. His
Button-like eyes move into motion.
The frog slithers from his resting place.

Richard Alan Pierce, aged 10

Sunday Dip

The morning road is thronged with merry boys
Who seek the water for their Sunday joys;
They run to seek the shallow pit, and wade
And dance about the water in the shade.
The boldest ventures first and dashes in,
And others go and follow to the chin,
And duck about, and try to lose their fears,
And laugh to hear the thunder in their ears.
They bundle up the rushes for a boat
And try across the deepest place to float:
Beneath the willow trees they ride and stoop –
The awkward load will scarcely bear them up.
  Without their aid the others float away,
  And play about the water half the day.

John Clare

WHAT TO DO

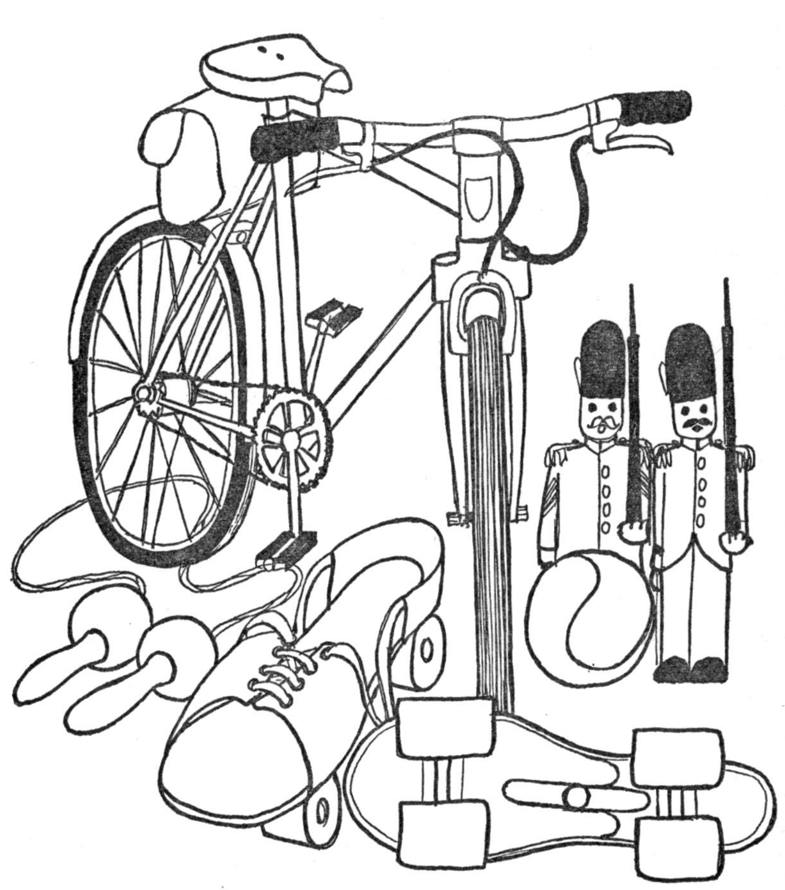

Going Downhill on a Bicycle: A Boy's Song

With lifted feet, hands still,
I am poised, and down the hill
Dart, with heedful mind;
The air goes by in a wind.

Swifter and yet more swift,
Till the heart with a mighty lift
Makes the lungs laugh, the throat cry:—
'Oh bird, see; see, bird, I fly.'

'Is this, is this your joy?
O bird, then I, though a boy,
For a golden moment share
Your feathery life in air!'

Say, heart, is there aught like this
In a world that is full of bliss?
'Tis more than skating, bound
Steel-shod to the level ground.

Speed slackens now, I float
Awhile in my airy boat;
Till, when the wheels scarce crawl,
My feet to the treadles fall.

Alas, that the longest hill
Must end in a vale; but still,
Who climbs with toil, wheresoe'er,
Shall find wings waiting there.

Henry Charles Beeching

Skipping

Little children skip,
The rope so gaily gripping,
   Tom and Harry,
   Jane and Mary,
   Kate, Diana,
   Susan, Anna,
All are fond of skipping!

The grasshoppers all skip,
The early dew-drop sipping,
   Under, over
   Bent and clover,
   Daisy, sorrel,
   Without quarrel,
All are fond of skipping!

The little boats they skip,
Beside the heavy shipping,
   And while the squalling
   Winds are calling,
   Falling, rising,
   Rising, falling,
All are fond of skipping!

The autumn leaves they skip,
When blasts the trees are stripping;
  Bounding, whirling,
  Sweeping, twirling,
  And in wanton
  Mazes curling,
All are fond of skipping!

Thomas Hood

A Cricket Triolet

I ran for a catch
  With the sun in my eyes, sir,
Being sure at a 'snatch',
I ran for a catch . . .
Now I wear a black patch,
and a nose such a size, sir,
I ran for a catch
  With the sun in my eyes, sir.

C. Kernahan

Hide and Seek

Call out. Call loud: 'I'm ready! Come and find me!'
The sacks in the toolshed smell like the seaside.
They'll never find you in this salty dark,
But be careful that your feet aren't sticking out.
Wiser not to risk another shout.
The floor is cold. They'll probably be searching
The bushes near the swing. Whatever happens
You mustn't sneeze when they come prowling in.
And here they are, whispering at the door;
You've never heard them sound so hushed before.
Don't breathe. Don't move. Stay dumb. Hide in your blindness.
They're moving closer, someone stumbles, mutters;
Their words and laughter scuffle, and they're gone.
But don't come out just yet; they'll try the lane
And then the greenhouse and back here again.
They must be thinking that you're very clever,
Getting more puzzled as they search all over.
It seems a long time since they went away.
Your legs are stiff, the cold bites through your coat;
The dark damp smell of sand moves in your throat.
It's time to let them know that you're the winner.
Push off the sacks. Uncurl and stretch. That's better!
Out of the shed and call to them: 'I've won!
Here I am! Come and own up I've caught you!'
The darkening garden watches. Nothing stirs.
The bushes hold their breath; the sun is gone.
Yes, here you are. But where are they who sought you?

Vernon Scannell

The Boy Fishing

I am cold and alone,
On my tree-root sitting as still as stone.
The fish come to my net. I scorned the sun,
The voices on the road, and they have gone.
My eyes are buried in the cold pond, under
The cold, spread leaves; my thoughts are silver-wet.
I have ten stickleback, a half-day's plunder,
Safe in my jar. I shall have ten more yet.

E. J. Scovell

Canoe Story

We went in a long canoe, two of us.
He sat at the front, one of us.
I sat at the back, one of us.
We went in a long canoe, two of us.

Water whispered, 'I'm cool, ever so.'
Sun sang, 'I'm hot, hot.'
Breeze sighed, 'I'm not.'
Paddle said, 'Heave ho, ever so.'

He sat, his back to me, and paddled.
I sat, looked at his back, and dandled
My paddle on my knees, and dabbled
My hands, while he talked and babbled
And pushed and paddled and paddled, and paddled.

And paddled. And sweated. And puffed.
I was cool as the water.
He was hot as the sun.
He puffed, heave ho. I sighed, just so.

Sweating and puffing, he turned
And saw my paddle, at rest, on the floor, all alone,
My paddle, dry as a bone.
And he burst. He might have cursed.

He might have cursed, but I grabbed my paddle,
And I paddled and pushed, and poked and thrust,
And we skimmed, bubble-brimmed, across the lake,
While he sat and relaxed and cooled in the breeze.

And I gasped, 'It's hot.'
He smiled, 'I'm not.'
And I said, 'You look cool, ever so.'
And he turned and smiled, 'Heave ho, just so.'

Geoffrey Summerfield

The Circus

There's nothing quite like a circus –
We love it all.
The blare and flare and glitter,
The smells and sawdust and litter,
The big brass band noise.
Excited boys
Dream . . .
With a crack of a whip they tame lions,
Hold the tigers at bay,
Face the growling Polar bears . . .
A drum roll.
A man on a pole vaults,
Somersaults.
The audience sees
On the high trapeze
A scarlet figure swing, turn, and fall.
They hold their breath –
And he's caught!
Safe in the net!
The girls imagine themselves
In sequinned tights,
Swinging gracefully beneath the lights
Or riding that splendid,
Archingly beautiful,
White horse.
Suddenly, a hullaballoo of clowns:
Baggy trousered, long-nosed, painted,
They fall about amid a hurricane of pies,
Collapsing chairs and jets of water
Smack between the eyes!
Poodles, all yap and jump,
Spring through hoops.

Elephants, world-weary, lumber in,
Slow and patient,
Infinitely careful.
Trick cyclists and shiny seals,
Monkeys sharing messy meals,
Tumblers and conjurors,
And those who tempt the Fates
Spinning fragile plates. . . .
The Wild West finale comes too soon.
A gang of savage Redskins,
A covered wagon,
Shrieks, gun shots, clouds of acrid smoke
And in come the Rangers, just in time –
But too soon, oh! too soon!
For us!
There's nothing quite like a circus.
Greasepaint, sawdust, smells and tinsel.
We love it all.

Unknown

Any Excuse

Up and away
Up and away!
This fine Spring morning
Up and away!

It's early yet.
Curtain-patterned sunbeams
On the wall
Move
With gentle sway.
I'll watch and stay.
There's wind about.

Up and away
Up and away!
This fine Summer morning
Up and away!

It's early yet.
Clouds, black with golden tips
Lurk outside
Poised above the hill
Ready to boil over.
There's rain about.

Up and away
Up and away!
This fine Autumn morning
Up and away!

It's early yet.
Listen. The falling leaves
Whisper, sigh,
Too soon. Too soon.
We die. We die.
There's frost about.

Up and away
Up and away!
This fine Winter morning
Up and away!

It's early yet.
The heavy leaden sky,
Packed with cold,
Hangs
Above rooftops.
Feather flakes fall.
There's snow about.

Up and away
Up and away!
This fine bright morning!
Up and away?

No!
In bed
I'll stay.

T. H. Parker

Skating

When I try to skate,
My feet are so wary
They grit and they grate:
And then I watch Mary
Easily gliding,
Like an ice-fairy;
Skimming and curving,
Out and in,
With a turn of her head,
And a lift of her chin,
And a gleam of her eye,
And a twirl and a spin;
Sailing under
The breathless hush
Of the willows, and back
To the frozen rush;
Out to the island
And round the edge,
Skirting the rim
Of the crackling sedge,
Swerving close
To the poplar root,
And round the lake
On a single foot,
With a three, and an eight,
And a loop and a ring;
Where Mary glides,
The lake will sing!

Out in the mist
I hear her now
Under the frost
Of the willow-bough
Easily sailing,
Light and fleet,
With the song of the lake
Beneath her feet.

Herbert Asquith

The Little Red Sled

'Come out with me!' cried the little red sled.
'I'll give you the wings of a bird,' it said.
'The ground is all snowy;
The wind is all blowy!
We'll go like a fairy,
So light and so airy!'

Jocelyn Bush

SEASIDE

House of Sand

We knew it wouldn't last. That's why
We thumbed in turrets so prettily, fashioned doors
And windows, too, for small sand people to come

In and go out again – our little house,
Dark damp sand, driveway scored in, the sea
Encroaching upon our play.

        We watched it fall
Prey to grey water swirling, helped it on
With a good boot or two, stood by and smiled –

Our house of sand melts to a shapeless mound.

Philip Hobsbaum

maggie and milly and molly and may

maggie and milly and molly and may
went down to the beach(to play one day)

and maggie discovered a shell that sang
so sweetly she couldn't remember her troubles,and

milly befriended a stranded star
whose rays five languid fingers were;

and molly was chased by a horrible thing
which raced sideways while blowing bubbles:and

may came home with a smooth round stone
as small as a world and as large as alone.

For whatever we lose(like a you or a me)
it's always ourselves we find in the sea

e. e. cummings

Old Man Ocean

Old Man Ocean, how do you pound
Smooth glass rough, rough stones round?
Time and the tide and the wild waves rolling,
Night and the wind and the long grey dawn.

Old Man Ocean, what do you tell,
What do you sing in the empty shell?
Fog and the storm and the long bell tolling,
Bones in the deep and the brave men gone.

Russell Hoban

Little Johnny

Little Johnny fished all day,
Fishes would not come his way.
'Had enough of this,' said he,
'I'll be going home to tea!'

When the fishes saw him go,
Up they came all in a row;
Jumped about and laughed with glee,
Shouting, 'Johnny's gone to tea!'

Unknown

The Giant Crab

Along the steep wall at the old pier's side,
The scavenging crabs come up with the tide.
'Want to catch one? It's easy! You don't need a thing
But a stone, and some fish, and some odd bits of string;
Look here now – I'll show you. First fetch that big
  stone –
The one with the hole through – the cobbleshaped one;
Now join up your string – all the odd bits you've got –
Loop one end through the stone, and tie tight in a knot;
Then cram in these bits of stale fish for a bait . . .
Ready? Over she goes!
                    Now you've only to wait!'

Not long!

There's a tiny commotion below in the water;
There's a shout from above as the line becomes tauter;
There's a hauling up, hand over hand, until – whee-
  ee-ee! –
A monster-great crab swings clear of the sea –
All legs and sharp claws, hanging desperately on,
His pincers stuck fast through the hole in the stone!
'Quick, get him!' 'No hurry! He's stupid – he'll cling
Till we land him. Pull steady, and don't break the
  string,
Whoops! Over he comes! Give the string a sharp shake,
And he'll let go his hold and fall down on his back.'

Well done!

'Now who'll pick him up?' 'Not me!' 'No, not me!
It's you said you fancied a crab for your tea!'

'*I* said? *I* don't want him!' 'Hey, Billy, he's yours!
Come along and make friends with him!' 'What? With
those claws?
I'm not touching him yet; I'll wait till he's dead!'
'You boil them alive; that's what my mother said;
They scream in the saucepan.' 'This one would get out:
He'd flop on the floor and go scrambling about –
He'd crawl on the baby; he'd frighten the cat.
Why, he could do anything with claws like that!
He could jab you –'
'Hey, somebody! Lend me that stick:
Hook him by the legs and pitch him back quick!'
Whe-e-e-e-ew! Sploosh! He's gone . . .

Thank goodness!

John Walsh

Little Fan

'I don't like the look of little Fan, mother,
  I don't like her looks a little bit.
Her face – well, it's not exactly different,
  But there's something wrong with it.

'She went down to the sea-shore yesterday,
  And she talked to somebody there,
Now she won't do anything but sit
  And comb out her yellowy hair.

'Her eyes are shiny and she sings, mother,
  Like nobody ever sang before.
Perhaps they gave her something queer to eat,
  Down by the rocks on the shore.

'Speak to me, speak, little Fan dear,
  Aren't you feeling very well?
Where have you been and what are you singing,
  And what's that seaweedy smell?

'Where did you get that shiny comb, love,
  And those pretty coral beads so red?
Yesterday you had two legs, I'm certain,
  But now there's something else instead.

'I don't like the looks of little Fan, mother,
  You'd best go and close the door.
Watch now, or she'll be gone for ever
  To the rocks by the brown sandy shore.'

James Reeves

If Once You Have Slept on an Island

If once you have slept on an island
  You'll never be quite the same;
You may look as you looked the day before
  And go by the same old name,

You may bustle about in street and shop;
  You may sit at home and sew,
But you'll see blue water and wheeling gulls
  Wherever your feet may go.

You may chat to the neighbours of this and that
  And close to your fire keep,
But you'll hear ship whistle and lighthouse bell
  And tides beat through your sleep.

Oh, you won't know why, and you can't say how
  Such change upon you came,
But – once you have slept on an island
  You'll never be quite the same!

Rachel Field

Tree-Sleeping

When I was small and trees were high,
I loved to sleep out nights by the sea,
A spruce that held up half the sky
Had boughs like beds where I could lie,
So thick the twigs I could not slide
Through to earth, and at my side
The evening star lay close to me.

The night came over the ocean slow,
A wind came up from nowhere there,
I felt my tree go to and fro
Until my bed was wholly air,
I lay on music grave and deep
Moved on oceans of holy sleep,
With great stars tangled in my hair.

A sea-bird on a snowy wing
Came down with treble cries,
Alighted on my bed, this thing
Woke me with wide surprise,
Flew off with golden talons curled,
And there on the blue edge of the world
The young sun looked me in the eyes.

Robert P. Tristram Coffin

PETS

Mick

Mick my mongrel-O
Lives in a bungalow,
Painted green with a round doorway.
With an eye for cats
And a nose for rats
He lies on his threshold half the day.
He buries his bones
By the rockery stones,
And never, oh never, forgets the place.
Ragged and thin
From his tail to his chin,
He looks at you with a sideways face.
Dusty and brownish,
Wicked and clownish,
He'll win no prize at the County Show.
But throw him a stick,
And up jumps Mick,
And right through the flower-beds see him go!

James Reeves

I Held a Lamb

One day when I went visiting,
A little lamb was there,
I picked it up and held it tight,
It didn't seem to care.
Its wool was soft and felt so warm –
Like sunlight on the sand,
And when I gently put it down
It licked me on the hand.

Kim Worthington

Anne and the Fieldmouse

We found a mouse in the chalk quarry today
In a circle of stones and empty oil drums
By the fag end of a fire. There had been
A picnic there: he must have been after the crumbs.

Jane saw him first, a flicker of brown fur
In and out of the charred wood and chalk-white.
I saw him last, but not till we'd turned up
Every stone and surprised him into flight,

Though not far – little zigzag spurts from stone
To stone. Once, as he lurked in his hiding-place,
I saw his beady eyes uplifted to mine.
I'd never seen such terror in so small a face.

I watched, amazed and guilty. Beside us suddenly
A heavy pheasant whirred up from the ground,
Scaring us all; and, before we knew it, the mouse
Had broken cover, skimming away without a sound,

Melting into the nettles. We didn't go
Till I'd chalked in capitals on a rusty can:
THERE'S A MOUSE IN THOSE NETTLES. LEAVE
HIM ALONE. NOVEMBER 15th. ANNE.

Ian Serraillier

My Brother Bert

Pets are the Hobby of my brother Bert.
He used to go to school with a Mouse in his shirt.

His Hobby it grew, as some hobbies will,
And grew and GREW and GREW until –

Oh don't breathe a word, pretend you haven't heard.
A simply appalling thing has occurred –

The very thought makes me iller and iller:
Bert's brought home a gigantic Gorilla!

If you think that's really not such a scare,
What if it quarrels with his Grizzly Bear?

You still think you could keep your head?
What if the Lion from under the bed

And the four Ostriches that deposit
Their football eggs in his bedroom closet

And the Aardvark out of his bottom drawer
All danced out and joined in the Roar?

What if the Pangolins were to caper
Out of their nests behind the wallpaper?

With the fifty sorts of Bats
That hang on his hatstand like old hats,

And out of a shoebox the excitable Platypus
Along with the Ocelot or Jungle-Cattypus?

The Wombat, the Dingo, the Gecko, the Grampus –
How they would shake the house with their Rumpus!

Not to forget the Bandicoot
Who would certainly peer from his battered old boot.

Why it would be a dreadful day,
And what Oh what would the neighbours say!

Ted Hughes

SEASONS

High

Fly, Kite!
High!
Till you touch the sky!
Stoop, whistling in the wind;
And whisper down the quivering string
If, as you soar, you find
The world we tread is like a ball –
With mounds for hills, and ponds for seas,
Its oxen small as creeping bees,
Mere bushes its huge trees!
But ah, the dew begins to fall,
The evening star to shine,
Down you must sink to earth again –
An earth, I mean, like mine.

Walter de la Mare

The Piper

A piper in the streets today
Set up and tuned, and started to play,
And away, away, away on the tide
Of his music we started; on every side
Doors and windows were opened wide,
And men left down their work and came,
And women with petticoats coloured like flame,
And little bare feet that were blue with cold,
Went dancing back to the age of gold,
And all the world went gay, went gay,
For half an hour in the street today.

Seamus O'Sullivan

Day by Day I Float My Paper Boats

Day by day I float my paper boats one by one down the running stream.
In big black letters I write my name on them and the name of the village where I live.
I hope that someone in some strange land will find them and know who I am.
I load my little boats with shiuli flowers from our garden, and hope that these blooms of the dawn will be carried safely to land in the night . . .

Rabindranath Tagore

The Calendar

I knew when spring was come –
Not by the murmurous hum
Of bees in the willow trees,
Or frills
Of daffodils,
Or the scent of the breeze;
But because there were whips and tops
By the jars of lollipops
In the two little village shops.

I knew when summer breathed –
Not by the flowers that wreathed
The sedge by the water's edge,
Or gold
Of the wold,
Or white and rose of the hedge;
But because, in a wooden box
In the window at Mrs. Mock's,
There were white-winged shuttlecocks.

I knew when autumn came –
Not by the crimson flame
Of leaves that lapped the eaves
Or mist
In amethyst
And opal-tinted weaves;
But because there were alley-taws
(Punctual as hips and haws)
On the counter at Mrs. Shaw's.

I knew when winter swirled –
Not by the whitened world,
Or silver skeins in the lanes
Or frost
That embossed
Its patterns on window panes:
But because there were transfer-sheets
By the bottles of spice and sweets
In the shops in two little streets.

Barbara Euphan Todd

Nurse's Song

When the voices of children are heard on the green
And laughing is heard on the hill,
My heart is at rest within my breast
  And everything else is still.

'Then come home, my children, the sun is gone down
And the dews of night arise;
Come, come, leave off play, and let us away
Till the morning appears in the skies.'

'No, no, let us play, for it is yet day
And we cannot go to sleep;
Besides, in the sky the little birds fly
And the hills are all cover'd with sheep.'

'Well, well, go and play till the light fades away
And then go home to bed.'
The little ones leaped and shouted and laugh'd
  And all the hills echoed.

William Blake

The Hollow Tree

How oft a summer shower hath started me
To seek for shelter in a hollow tree –
Old huge ash dotterel wasted to a shell
Whose vigorous head still grew and flourished well,
Where ten might sit upon the battered floor
And still look round discovering room for more
And he who chose a hermit life to share
Might have a door and make a cabin there.
They seemed so like a house that our desires
Would call them so and make our gipsy fires
And eat field dinners of the juicy peas
Till we were wet and drabbled to the knees,
But in our old tree house rain as it might
Not one drop fell although it rained till night.

John Clare

I Meant to Do My Work Today

I meant to do my work today –
But a brown bird sang in the apple tree,
And a butterfly flitted across the field,
And all the leaves were calling me.

And the wind went sighing over the land,
Tossing the grasses to and fro,
And a rainbow held out its shining hand –
So what could I do but laugh and go?

Richard le Gallienne

Heat Wave

Where am I?
Lying, drowning in glorious heat,
My body floats towards the sun
Returns in a cool breeze.
My eyes close,
A glow from nowhere out of darkness
Blinds my eyelids.
I get hotter, I fill with the heat,
I could sleep on and on;
The heat hypnotizes my sun drenched mind.

Falling deeper into the heat
The damp grass irritates me
Clings to my sweating skin.

The wind licks my arms and legs
My hair rushes with it.

Here I am
Drowning peacefully,
Browning hopefully,
The sun overcoming my body,
I sleep on . . .

Valerie Hodge, aged 14

Rain in Summer

How beautiful is the rain!
After the dust and heat,
In the broad and fiery street,
In the narrow lane,
How beautiful is the rain!
How it clatters along the roofs,
Like the tramp of hoofs!

How it gushes and struggles out
From the throat of the overflowing spout!
Across the window pane
It pours and pours;
And swift and wide,
With a muddy tide,
Like a river down the gutter roars
The rain, the welcome rain!

H. W. Longfellow

Meeting

As I went home on the old wood road,
  With my basket and lesson book,
A deer came out of the tall trees
  And down to drink at the brook.

Twilight was all about us,
  Twilight and tree on tree;
I looked straight into its great, strange eyes,
  And the deer looked back at me.

Beautiful, brown, and unafraid,
  Those eyes returned my stare;
And something with neither sound nor name
  Passed between us there.

Something I shall not forget –
  Something still, and shy, and wise –
In the dimness of the woods
  From a pair of gold-flecked eyes.

Rachel Field

The Hayloft

Through all the pleasant meadow-side
The grass grew shoulder-high,
Till the shining scythes went far and wide
And cut it down to dry.

These green and sweetly smelling crops
They led in waggons home;
And they piled them here in mountaintops
For mountaineers to roam.

Here is Mount Clear, Mount Rusty-Nail,
Mount Eagle and Mount High:
The mice that in these mountains dwell
No happier are than I!

O what a joy to clamber there,
O what a place for play,
With the sweet, the dim, the dusty air;
The happy hills of hay.

Robert Louis Stevenson

Five O'Clock Tea

Outside the cold winds blow,
The snow comes pelting down.
It is five o'clock and the sun is setting.
But inside the fire is roaring,
The kettle is whistling,
The fat is bubbling,
And the oven roaring.
The gas bangs as it goes out.
There is a clash as the plates are put down.
The potatoes being served send off clouds of steam.
Then there is the ring of a bell
And a shout calling, 'Tea's ready'.
The food comes in amidst a cloud of steam.

Steven Willett, aged 9

Halloween

'Granny, I saw a witch go by,
I saw two, I saw three!
I heard their skirts go swish, swish, swish –'

'Child, 'twas leaves against the sky,
And the autumn wind in the tree.'

'Granny, broomsticks they bestrode,
Their hats were black as tar,
And buckles twinkled on their shoes –'

'You saw but shadows on the road,
The sparkle of a star.'

'Granny, all their heels were red,
Their cats were big as sheep.
I heard a bat say to an owl – '

'Child, you must go straight to bed,
'Tis time you were asleep.'

'Granny, I saw men in green,
Their eyes shone fiery red,
Their heads were yellow pumpkins – '

'Now you've told me what you've seen,
WILL you go to bed?'

'Granny?'

'Well?'

'Don't you believe –?'

'What?'

'What I've seen?
Don't you know it's Halloween?'

Marie A. Lawson

Birches *(an extract)*

When I see birches bend to left and right
Across the lines of straighter darker trees,
I like to think some boy's been swinging them.
But swinging doesn't bend them down to stay
As ice-storms do. Often you must have seen them
Loaded with ice a sunny winter morning
After a rain. They click upon themselves
As the breeze rises, and turn many-coloured
As the stir cracks and crazes their enamel.
Soon the sun's warmth makes them shed crystal shells
Shattering and avalanching on the snow-crust –
Such heaps of broken glass to sweep away
You'd think the inner dome of heaven had fallen.
They are dragged to the withered bracken by the load,
And they seem not to break; though once they are bowed
So low for long, they never right themselves:
You may see their trunks arching in the woods
Years afterwards, trailing their leaves on the ground
Like girls on hands and knees that throw their hair
Before them over their heads to dry in the sun.

Robert Frost

A Child's Voice

On winter nights shepherd and I
  Down to the lambing shed would go;
Rain round our swinging lamp did fly
  Like shining flakes of snow.

There on a nail our lamp we hung,
  And O it was beyond belief
To see those ewes lick with hot tongues
  The limp wet lambs to life.

A week gone and sun shining warm
  It was as good as gold to hear
Those new-born voices round the farm
  Cry shivering and clear.

Where was a prouder man than I
  Who knew the night those lambs were born
Watching them leap two feet on high
  And stamp the ground in scorn?

Gone sheep and shed and lighted rain
  And blue March morning; yet today
A small voice crying brings again
  Those lambs leaping at play.

Andrew Young

WISHES

There Isn't Time

There isn't time, there isn't time
  To do the things I want to do –
With all the mountain tops to climb
  And all the woods to wander through
And all the seas to sail upon,
  And everywhere there is to go,
And all the people, every one,
  Who live upon the earth to know.
There's only time, there's only time
To know a few, to do a few,
  And then sit down and make a rhyme
    About the rest I want to do.

Eleanor Farjeon

Travel

I should like to rise and go
Where the golden apples grow; –
Where below another sky
Parrot islands anchored lie,
And, watched by cockatoos and goats,
Lonely Crusoes building boats; –
Where in sunshine reaching out
Eastern cities, miles about,
Are with mosque and minaret
Among sandy gardens set,
And rich goods from near and far
Hang for sale in the bazaar; –
Where the Great Wall round China goes,
And on one side the desert blows,
And with bell and voice and drum,
Cities on the other hum; –
Where are forests, hot as fire,
Wide as England, tall as a spire,
Full of apes and cocoa-nuts
And the negro hunters' huts; –
Where the knotty crocodile
Lies and blinks in the Nile,
And the red flamingo flies
Hunting fish before his eyes; –
Where in jungles, near and far,
Man-devouring tigers are,
Lying close and giving ear
Lest the hunt be drawing near,
Or a comer-by be seen
Swinging in a palanquin; –
Where among the desert sands
Some deserted city stands,

All its children, sweep and prince,
Grown to manhood ages since,
Not a foot in street or house,
Not a stir of child or mouse,
And when kindly falls the night,
In all the town no spark of light.
There I'll come when I'm a man
With a camel caravan;
Light a fire in the gloom
Of some dusty dining-room;
See the pictures on the walls,
Heroes, fights, and festivals;
And in a corner find the toys
Of the old Egyptian boys.

Robert Louis Stevenson

I Wish I Were . . .

When the gong sounds at ten in the morning and I walk to school by our lane,
Every day I meet the hawker crying, 'Bangles, crystal bangles!'
There is nothing to hurry him on, there is no road he must take, no place he must go to, no time when he must come home.
I wish I were a hawker, spending my day in the road, crying, 'Bangles, crystal bangles!'

When at four in the afternoon I come back from the school,
I can see through the gate of that house the gardener digging the ground.
He does what he likes with his spade, he soils his clothes with the dust,
Nobody takes him to task if he gets baked in the sun or gets wet.
I wish I were a gardener digging away at the garden with nobody to stop me from digging.
Just as it gets dark in the evening and my mother sends me to bed,
I can see through my open window the watchman walking up and down.
The lane is dark and lonely, and the street-lamp stands
Like a giant with one red eye in its head.

The watchman swings his lantern and walks with his
shadow at his side, and never once goes to bed in his
life.
I wish I were a watchman walking the streets all night,
chasing the shadows with my lantern.

Rabindranath Tagore

It Was Long Ago

I'll tell you, shall I, something I remember?
Something that still means a great deal to me.
It was long ago.

A dusty road in summer I remember,
A mountain, and an old house, and a tree
That stood, you know,

Behind the house. An old woman I remember,
In a red shawl with a grey cat on her knee
Humming under a tree.

She seemed the oldest thing I can remember,
But then perhaps I was not more than three.
It was long ago.

I dragged on the dusty road, and I remember
How the old woman looked over the fence at me
And seemed to know

How it felt to be three, and called out, I remember
'Do you like bilberries and cream for tea?'
I went under the tree

And while she hummed, and the cat purred, I remember
How she filled a saucer with berries and cream for me
So long ago,

Such berries and such cream as I remember
I never had seen before, and never see
Today, you know.

And that is almost all I can remember,
The house, the mountain, the grey cat on her knee,
Her red shawl, and the tree,

And the taste of the berries, the feel of the sun I
remember,
And the smell of everything that used to be
So long ago,

Till the heat on the road outside again I remember,
And how the long dusty road seemed to have for me
No end, you know.

That is the farthest thing I can remember.
It won't mean much to you. It does to me.
Then I grew up, you see.

Eleanor Farjeon

Index of Authors

Index of First Lines

In the same series:

The Swinging Rainbow

Poems for the Young

Selected by Howard Sergeant

Funny and thoughtful, long and short – this book contains many kinds of poems: poems that tell stories and those that create pictures in the mind; poems to appeal to a sense of adventure, and poems about everyday things. It is a collection to be read and enjoyed again and again and there is something in it for everyone.

Happy Landings

Poems for the Youngest

Chosen by Howard Sergeant

A happy mixture of old favourites and modern poems, this collection has been specially chosen to appeal to very young children. But to listen to or to read, this is a delightful new anthology which opens all children's minds to the strange new world of poetry.

Come Follow Me

Poems for everyone

A lively and interesting collection of poems for young children which has already delighted thousands of readers all over the world.